Look!

Written by Cindy Chapman
Illustrated by Esther Szegedy

Scholastic Inc.

**New York Toronto London Auckland Sydney
Mexico City New Delhi Hong Kong**

ISBN 0-439-17364-7

20 19 18 17 16 15 14 10 11 12

Printed in the U.S.A. 23

First Scholastic clubs printing, January 2000

Look!
The dogs are in the tub.

Look!

The dogs are in the garden.

Look!
The dogs are in the truck.

Look!

The dogs are in the water.

Look!
The dogs are in the mud.

Look!

The dogs are in the sand.

Look!
The dogs are in the tub.